STATES OF MIND

I FEEL BORED

BY STEPHANIE FINNE

BLUE OWL
BOOKS

TIPS FOR CAREGIVERS

Social and emotional learning (SEL) helps children manage emotions, create and achieve goals, maintain relationships, learn how to feel empathy, and make good decisions. The SEL approach will help children establish positive habits in communication, cooperation, and decision-making. By incorporating SEL in early reading, children will be better equipped to build confidence and foster positive peer networks.

BEFORE READING

Talk to the reader about boredom. Boredom can be a sign of other feelings.

Discuss: What does it feel like when you are bored? What other feelings do you feel? What do you do when you feel bored?

AFTER READING

Talk to the reader about ways to cultivate creativity. Explain that being bored helps us be creative. It helps us find what we enjoy and can also help us learn how to make our own choices.

Discuss: How often do you feel bored? What can you do?
Can you set aside one night a week for a new activity?

SEL GOAL

Some students may struggle with boredom because they have trouble focusing. They may be expressing many other feelings that they haven't been able to identify. Help them find words for their inner experiences and states of mind through books, visuals, and other resources.

TABLE OF CONTENTS

CHAPTER 1

FEELING BORED

Have you ever been bored? How did that feel? Were you tired and unable to **focus**? Did you want to do something different?

We feel bored when we aren't interested in something. Boredom can happen at home or at school. It can even happen when we are doing something fun! Sometimes we just aren't interested in an activity.

Boredom looks different for everyone. Some people **yawn**. Some stare or **daydream**.

Others can't sit still. They have too much **energy**. They may act out. Mark gets bored in the car. He picks on his little sister.

PASS THE TIME

If you are somewhere for a long period of time, find a game you can play. This can help pass the time.

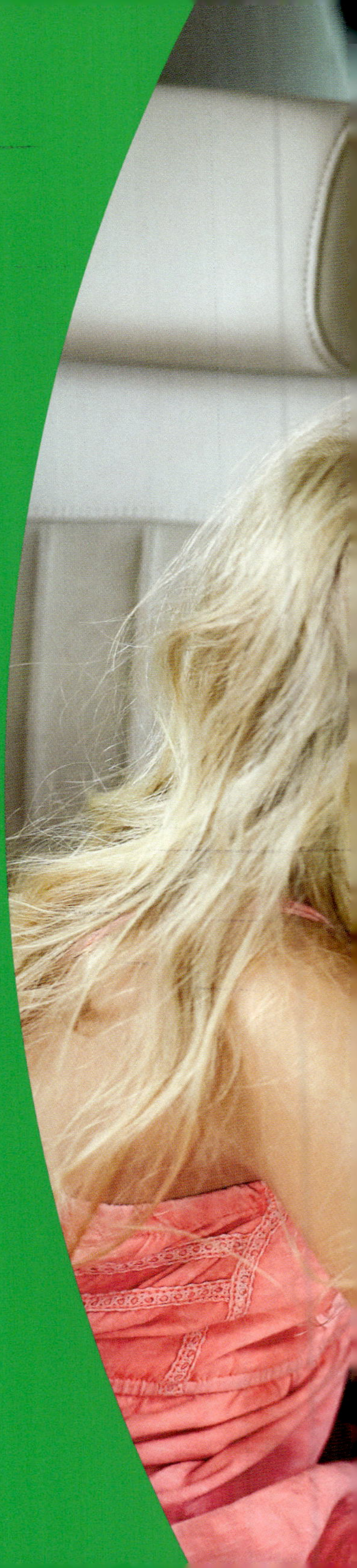

CHAPTER 2

WHAT CAN YOU DO?

Being bored can be **frustrating**. When you don't find an activity interesting, it can be hard to focus. You want to do something else. When you can't, you may get angry. So what can you do?

Try doing something active! When Abby is bored at home, she asks her neighbor to play outside. They take turns thinking of new games!

fidget spinner

You can't do whatever you want in school. Even if you are not interested in a subject, you still need to listen.

Benji takes notes with different colored pens. If Maren finishes a test early, she quietly plays with her fidget spinner. It helps her release energy.

BE AWARE

Just because you are bored doesn't mean others are. Think before you act. Will your actions bother those around you?

If you are bored often, try writing down your feelings. Think about what is making you bored. Then **brainstorm** ideas. What could you do to feel **engaged**?

Make a list of activities you like to do at home. Think about ways you can join in lessons at school. Write your ideas down.

ASK FOR HELP

Talk to a parent or teacher if you are feeling bored often. Ask them to help you brainstorm ideas.

AT HOME:

- build a pillow fort
- play tag
- set up a pretend store

AT SCHOOL:

- use different colored pencils
- make a list of questions to ask about the lesson
- use a quiet fidget

IN PUBLIC:

- find shapes in things around me
- bring a coloring book and markers
- count the number of people around me

Try a new activity. It can be scary to try something new, but it can also feel good. It is OK to make mistakes. Keep trying. Learning something new is never boring!

Exercise helps Tia focus. She was nervous to try out for the team, but she loves practice! She is making new friends, too!

Practice being **mindful**. This helps us be in the moment and appreciate what is happening right now. Close your eyes. What do you hear and smell? How does your body feel?

MINDFULNESS EXERCISE

Try the S.T.O.P. exercise:

- Stop what you are doing.
- Take a breath.
- **Observe**. Take note of what is happening. How do you feel?
- **Proceed**. After you take a moment, keep going!

CHAPTER 3

SHARING SPACE

Everyone gets bored sometimes. Mel doesn't get mad when her brother gets bored. Instead, she suggests a new game. They find something else to play.

Set **goals** with your friends, or help them set their own. Micah's goal is to try a new recipe.

Some new choices or goals don't feel right. That's OK. It happens! Think about what you could do differently next time. It feels really good when you find a new activity you enjoy. What will you do the next time you feel bored?

GOALS AND TOOLS

GROW WITH GOALS

We can all feel bored sometimes. What we do to find other options can make a big difference to the people around us. It can feel good when we make a positive change.

Goal: Identify what boredom feels like. How do you feel when you are bored? How do you usually react to being bored?

Goal: Brainstorm activities you can do. Write down a list of things you would like to do. Write whatever comes to mind.

Goal: Think about how your options would affect others. Will your chosen activity disrupt your class? Will you be helping someone else with your new activity? Can you include others in your activity?

MINDFULNESS EXERCISE

Feeling bored can make it difficult to make good decisions. It can sometimes lead to acting out. Here are some steps to help you be mindful and choose something else to do:

1. Stop and breathe.
2. Identify your choices.
3. Consider your options.
4. Make a choice and do it.
5. Think about how it went.

GLOSSARY

brainstorm
To come up with ideas or solutions to a problem.

daydream
To let your mind wander and imagine things.

energy
The ability or strength to do things without getting tired.

engaged
Greatly interested and involved.

focus
To concentrate on something.

frustrating
Causing feelings of anger and annoyance.

goals
Things you aim to do.

mindful
A mentality achieved by focusing on the present moment and calmly recognizing and accepting your feelings, thoughts, and sensations.

observe
To watch someone or something closely, especially to learn something.

proceed
To move forward or continue.

yawn
To open your mouth wide and breathe in deeply, especially because you are tired or bored.

TO LEARN MORE

FACT SURFER

Finding more information is as easy as 1, 2, 3.

1. Go to www.factsurfer.com
2. Enter "**Ifeelbored**" into the search box.
3. Choose your cover to see a list of websites.

INDEX

Blue Owl Books are published by Jump!, 5357 Penn Avenue South, Minneapolis, MN 55419, www.jumplibrary.com

Library of Congress Cataloging-in-Publication Data

Names: Finne, Stephanie, author.
Title: I feel bored / Stephanie Finne.
Description: Minneapolis, MN: Jump!, Inc., [2021] | Series: States of mind
Includes index. | Audience: Ages 7–10 | Audience: Grades 2–3
Identifiers: LCCN 2019046378 (print)
LCCN 2019046379 (ebook)
ISBN 9781645273981 (hardcover)
ISBN 9781645273998 (paperback)
ISBN 9781645274001 (ebook)
Subjects: LCSH: Boredom—Juvenile literature. | Emotions in children—Juvenile literature.
Classification: LCC BF575.B67 F56 2021 (print)
LCC BF575.B67 (ebook) | DDC 152.4–dc23
LC record available at https://lccn.loc.gov/2019046378
LC ebook record available at https://lccn.loc.gov/2019046379

Editor: Jenna Gleisner
Designer: Molly Ballanger

Photo Credits: LightField Studios/Shutterstock, cover; AvailableLight/iStock, 1; Krakenimages.com/Shutterstock, 3; Khwanchai_s/Shutterstock, 4; David Prado Perucha/Shutterstock, 5; Robert Kneschke/Shutterstock, 6–7; Happy Together/Shutterstock, 8; kirin_photo/iStock, 9; R-Tvist/iStock, 10–11; photka/Shutterstock, 12–13; SDI Productions/iStock, 14–15; brusinski/iStock, 16–17 (foreground); mediaphotos/iStock, 16–17 (background); Dean Mitchell/iStock, 18; kate_sept2004/iStock, 19; Jupiterimages/Getty, 20–21.

Printed in the United States of America at Corporate Graphics in North Mankato, Minnesota.